She Can She Will She Wins

Mask Off

Donna Floyd

Donna Floyd
She Can She Will She Wins
Mask Off

Donna Floyd
She Can She Will She Wins
Mask Off

Copyright © 2019 by Donna Floyd

All rights reserved. No part of this book may be used or reproduced in any manner whatsoever without the written permission of the publisher, except where permitted by law. Any similarities to persons living or dead is purely coincidental.

Cover Design: DH Publishing Company
ISBN: 13: 978-1-7336502-0-5
ISBN: 10: 1-7336502-0-2
Edited: DH Publishing Company
www.dhpublishingco.com
dhpublishingco@gmail.com
Author: donnaperfectfit0566@yahoo.com

Donna Floyd
She Can She Will She Wins
Mask Off

Donna Floyd
She Can She Will She Wins
Mask Off

In loving memory of my son Antonio Jackson, brother Anthony Jackson, and Deangelo Brown, Antonio, I love you, and because of you, I'm no longer afraid to be who God has called me to be. You have helped me with the vision of Hiding Behind the Mask. After your death, my mask of fear came off. I am no longer afraid. God told me since you are no longer afraid, it's time for you to be a blessing to others and to help them shed their mask. Thank you.

Donna Floyd
She Can She Will She Wins
Mask Off

Donna Floyd
She Can She Will She Wins
Mask Off

CONTENT

Acknowledgement............................... 9

About the Author............................... 11

Introduction…………………………….. 13

Chapter One-Unforgiving Mask............ 17

Chapter Two-Insecurity....................... 25

Chapter Three-Depression................... 31

Chapter Four-Addiction...................... 37

Chapter Five-Abuse........................... 41

Chapter Six-Loss of a Loved One............ 46

Chapter Seven-Fear........................... 53

Final-How to Shed Your Mask............ 59

Donna Floyd
She Can She Will She Wins
Mask Off

Donna Floyd
She Can She Will She Wins
Mask Off

Acknowledgements

Throughout my life, I've encountered many people who have helped to propel me to my destiny. If you are reading this book, you are one of them. Thank you. Giving thanks first to my Lord and Savior because without him none of this would have been possible. Second, to my wonderful husband Shawn Floyd, thanks for being my support, provider, and protector. To my family and friends, may God continue to bless each one of you. This book is dedicated to everyone that has experienced difficult life circumstances. My prayer is that you realize that under the mask lay the real you. You are somebody, you're complete, fearfully, and wonderfully made just as God created you. May you be encouraged to remove the mask and walk boldly in God's perfect plan for your life. Mask Off.

Sincerely, Donna Floyd

Donna Floyd
She Can She Will She Wins
Mask Off

Donna Floyd
She Can She Will She Wins
Mask Off

ABOUT THE AUTHOR

L**ady** Donna Floyd was born to mother Bernella, and father Starling. She was raised in Indianapolis, Indiana and grew up on the south side of town, with three brothers and two sisters. Donna attended Thomas Carr Howe High School, where she graduated in 1984. After high school, Donna moved to California to pursue a modeling career. Years later, she returned home and attended Ivy Tech Community College.

In 1998 she started pursuing the Lord and met the love of her life Shawn Floyd. Shawn and Donna tied the knot in 1999. Donna has 13 children (Blended family) she has four biological children, two boys, and two girls and she is also a grandmother.

Donna started sewing in leadership roles, not only in the church, but outside the ministry. She was called to the ministry in 2008 and realized this was her calling.

In 2014, she launched her first conference, calling all women to unite.

In 2015, God gave her the Vision Hiding behind the Mask conference, allowing women to know who they are in Christ Jesus. She launched her conference in March 2016.

In 2016, she wrote her first book Hiding Behind the Mask the Deliverance. In the same year, she and her husband launched a church called New Christian

Donna Floyd
She Can She Will She Wins
Mask Off

Hope. They also have a ministry feeding the community.
This is Donna's second book She Can, She Will, She Wins, Mask Off.

Donna Floyd
She Can She Will She Wins
Mask Off

Introduction

Who are you? For most of my life, I struggled with who God created me to be. The struggle was allowing others to make me feel like I wasn't good enough. I let the fear of what others thought to immobilize me. As a result, I lived in regret and resentment. Most of my life I was naive, passive, and a people pleaser until the shackles came off. Now my knowledge of who I am in Christ empowers me to live out my purpose.

On Valentine's Day, Feb 2015, I lost my beloved son. His untimely death removed any fears that still lingered in my mind. I know this may be the complete opposite for many, but my relationship with God has taught me that God will allow situations and circumstances to happen in our life to launch us deeper into his will. My son's death is not in vain, and everything I wished I had done for him, I can now do for others. God is using me to make a difference in others lives.

Who are you? What mask do you wear? Depression, Fear, Insecurities, Hurt, Loss of a loved one. Why is it that we only allow others to see the outside, but not what's deep down on the inside. A lot of times we hide behind the mask because of fear of what others may think or find out about us. The mask can be

Donna Floyd
She Can She Will She Wins
Mask Off

harmful and a sign of weakness. Sometimes we can be emotionally disconnected, and that can wear you out until you can be a witness to your pain and speak it. That's when the healing begins. You can be free and healed. That's when true self emerges. Healing of knowing who we are in Christ Jesus. We can choose to hide behind our mask or open ourselves up and take off the Mask.

Like I said before, my mask was fear, false evidence appearing real. I allowed fear to immobilize me. I was not myself. I allow others to dictate who I was. I didn't have an opinion, but I allowed others to control me. I was a yes woman. The mask was fear and insecurity of hiding behind my real beauty. Today my mask is removed and as you read in the fear chapter a little bit of my story is told. Don't be ashamed of who you used to be but know who you are in Christ. Tell others your story; it may make a difference in someone's life. I stand tall now, God has brought me a long way from being a passive girl and now being used for his glory.

I will continue to promote women by letting them know the mask is not who we represent; it's a misrepresentation of who we think we are. Don't spend another day trying to live in your strength. When we tell our story, we get comfort from healing and restoration. We can't fully heal until we let go and give ourselves wholly to who we are and then we can put the pieces back together. We were not born with a mask. You have the power to change your situation because greatness lives in you. Don't be afraid of change; God has a new beginning for you,

Donna Floyd
She Can She Will She Wins
Mask Off

trust the process. The greatest battle we have as humans is worrying about what the world thinks about us. But God doesn't see you as others do, because he looks at our heart. We can learn to be ourselves and take off the mask. As you read the journey of my life, you will see the healing process. I've told my story so that it may touch someone's life. It's ok to speak the truth because that is who I used to be, but greatness lives in me. Don't give up, keep pressing, you are somebody. Never hesitate to ask God for radical changes. He can, He will, and You win. We have a living hope in Christ; we have victory behind the mask. You Can You Will You Win. It's time to shed our mask.

As you continue to read my book, you will learn that I have worn all seven mask and I am not ashamed. I've been healed and delivered because I know who I am in Christ Jesus. Won't he do it!
At the end of my book, it will tell you three reasons why we should discard our mask.

Donna Floyd
She Can She Will She Wins
Mask Off

Donna Floyd
She Can She Will She Wins
Mask Off

Chapter One
Unforgiving Mask

The reason I started with the unforgiving Mask is that it's one of the most prominent masks that we wear, and we don't even realize it. We cannot have peace with God and at the same time have an unforgiving spirit with others. Romans 8:6| To be spiritually minded is life and peace. Daily we must consciously choose to center our lives around God. Sometimes, you have to ask yourself, what would Jesus want me to do?
Our relationship with others must be correct before our relationship with God can be. We are running around here angry, bitter, and having an unforgiving spirit, allowing someone else to have power over us. It also stands in the way of God not answering our prayers or forgiving you. Mark 11:24| For this reason, I am telling you, whatever things you ask for in prayer, believe that you have received it and it will be given to you. Whenever you stand in prayer, if you have anything against anyone, forgive them, so that your father who is in heaven will also forgive you, but if you don't forgive, your heavenly father will neither forgive you or your transgressions.

As you read this Chapter today, ask yourself, is there anyone in my life that is in need of my forgiveness or if someone has wronged me, I need to forgive them today.

Donna Floyd
She Can She Will She Wins
Mask Off

An unforgiving spirit that we hide behind can destroy the joy of the Lord in our lives. We cover it up with our mask, and we wonder why we are always bitter or angry with others. The greatest joy in life is living in peace with God and our fellow men. This story that I will tell is a real example of how to live in peace when someone has wronged you.
This story is about a Father's forgiveness for his daughter. Now this is a true story, and if you think you have been through the storm, this story is inspiring, it helped me along the way. If you want to purchase the book, it's called Terror in the Night. About four years ago I went to visit this church here in Indianapolis, and at the time I was looking for a church home, and when I say God will speak to you through people, circumstances, and his word. This one particular day, I happen to visit this church the day the man came to talk about his book. He travels all over the world telling his story about forgiveness. Keep in mind that I was going through some things myself about forgiving others.
The speaker had a wife, two boys, and one teenage daughter. He was the Sunday school teacher at his church, and his family had always been at church. His daughter was reading the word and doing weekly activities in the church. One day she met a young man, which was older than she, probably about three years older and at the time, she was only 14. To make a long story short. Her parents allowed her to date this man until they started seeing different changes in her, so they told her that she could not see him anymore. The daughter and boyfriend ended up

Donna Floyd
She Can She Will She Wins
Mask Off

killing the mother, and the two brothers and tried to kill the Dad. The dad was shot five times, but he was able to get away and went to the neighbor's house for help. God saved the man so that he could tell his story and be a blessing to others who may have a hard time with forgiveness.
The daughter and boyfriend were arrested and charged with murder, but the most intriguing part about this story was in the courtroom, the father looked at the boyfriend and forgave him even though his wife and two sons were brutally murdered. To this day, he still visits his daughter in prison, and today she is ministering to people in prison about her story. The whole purpose of telling this story is to say that the man forgave after all the tragedy he experienced. Today he goes around the world preaching about forgiveness.

Let me help you and show you why we should forgive our enemies or those who have wronged us. Never take revenge in your own hands. Romans 12:19:21| Do not take revenge but leave room for the wrath of God, for it is written. It is mine to avenge; I will repay, says the Lord, but if your enemy is hungry, feed him and if he is thirsty, give him something to drink for in doing so, you will reap burning coal on his head (Love).
Do not be overcome by evil, but overcome evil with good. Forgiveness and compassion and by giving an enemy a drink, we're not excusing his misdeed, but recognizing them, and loving them in spite of it all, just as Christ did for us. Christ was nailed to the cross

Donna Floyd
She Can She Will She Wins
Mask Off

and said, forgive them, for they do not know what they are doing. Some people are less to be blamed and more to be taught. Here are three reasons why we should forgive:

1. Forgiveness breaks a cycle of retaliation.
2. Forgiving makes the person feel ashamed and will cause them to change their ways when we forgive.
3. Forgiving others will free you from a heavy load of bitterness.

You can't allow the enemy to have power over you. Take that power back by forgiving. Right actions lead to the right feelings. I am a witness to that statement. My prayers every day are: Please forgive those who sin against me and please forgive me if I've wronged them. Matthew 6:14| For if you forgive others of their sins, your heavenly Father will also forgive you. But if you do not forgive others, then your heavenly father will not forgive your trespasses. If we don't forgive others, we deny our common ground as sinners in need of God's forgiveness. It is easy to ask God for forgiveness, but when it comes to someone who has wronged us, we don't want to forgive. That's precisely why I pray that prayer every day. Ephesians 4:32| Be kind to one another, tenderhearted, and forgiving, just as God in Christ also has forgiven you. Love when others hate, give when others take, and help when others abuse. I had a friend that wronged me, yes, it was hurtful, and yes, I was angry at the time. I forgave her for what she had done. Keep in mind, she did not call to apologize, but

Donna Floyd
She Can She Will She Wins
Mask Off

because I know that Christ lives in me and Christ forgives, it was easy for me to overlook. I looked past her faults and viewed her as Christ would see us. He died, he forgave and gave up his life for us. So who are we not to forgive? I know some of you are saying, why are you forgiven her and she didn't apologize? That's the first thing that we think about, or I forgive, but I won't forget. But because of his mercy and grace that he shed upon us, we should want to be the image of Christ. No, we are not perfect, but we are to strive to be the image of Christ. Having to release forgiveness, we will pass it on to others. There will be a harvest of blessings waiting for you. Once again just recently, I saw her at a wedding, I haven't seen or spoken to her after I forgave her. So as I was walking to greet the bride, she came out first, and God spoke to me and said don't only talk to her but embrace her. When God speaks to you, do not harden your heart, but do what he says. So I did just that, I wrapped my arms around her. Giving God all the glory, but I thank God for allowing me to have a spirit of forgiveness. I had to take off the mask and put on love.
If God can wipe the slate clean and forgive others, how come we can't forgive others? Colossians 2:13| When we were dead in our sins, God made us alive together with Christ, having forgiven us of all our sins.

Over the last three years, I lost people that were dear to me, my son, brother, and son-in-law. My son-in-law died a horrible death. Because of the situation,

Donna Floyd
She Can She Will She Wins
Mask Off

sometimes it's hard to forgive someone who shows up in your front yard, shoots you and shoots at your cousin for no apparent reason other than jealousy. My son-in-law had just buried his dad and was at the repass at his house when the unexpected happened. I still can't come to grips with such nonsense, but I know we serve a God that says the battle is not yours but the Lords. He said I am the avenger leave room for his wrath. God will fight your battles. I forgive the shooter because God has the last say so.

With my son's situation, you all probably know that my son died of a drug overdose. I knew he was on drugs, but I was in denial. The night my son passed away, he died in the arms of his baby's mother. I had already known that he had passed before I got the call. My heart experienced pain like I had a heart attack, but while my heart was aching, his heart had stopped. That was three years ago on valentine's day. Just this past year, there was a rumor going around that someone had given my son some bad drugs. It doesn't matter because my son is all right now, no more drugs, worries, tears, everything is made new. To make a long story short, Satan wanted me to be upset, but what I did was, I prayed for the person and forgave the person because that's something he will have to live with for the rest of his life. My son is in a better place.
The world we live in is a cruel and sinful world that we live in and before my son passed away, he cried out to the lord and said help me Lord I'm about to die. He knew who to call on, and he knew his Savior.

Donna Floyd
She Can She Will She Wins
Mask Off

Today I can tell because of my son's death; my mask is off. Sometimes God will allow things to happen in your life to make you stronger and build up your character. Through all the trials and storms I've encountered with my loved one, I still forgive, and I thank God that I don't have a mask of an unforgiving Spirit.

Donna Floyd
She Can She Will She Wins
Mask Off

Chapter Two
Insecurity

One of my favorite scripture is 1st Timothy 4:4| For everything created is good, and nothing is to be rejected if it is received with thanksgiving. Being insecure means not feeling confident in yourself or a situation. It means doubting yourself or abilities. It can also mean feeling insecure or anxious and fearful about self. Insecurity can hold you back from what God has for you. I can speak about myself. After years of depression and going through life circumstances, I can say I've lost a lot of elasticity in my skin, especially my face, I look back at my pictures, and I wish I can look like that again. I felt my confidence going down the drain, doubting myself, feeling ashamed, and feeling unattractive. I would glance in the mirror and would cry. The person I was looking at back then wasn't there anymore in my eyes. I used to avoid eye contact with others or turn a certain way when I was talking to people and refused to take compliments from others. I felt so insecure that I doubted myself, not only in my looks but what God has called me to be. I had no backbone, but a wishbone. I was not confident in self. Once I knew who I was in Christ and what Christ thought about me, I can honestly say I am proud of the skin I am in today.
Psalms 139| God said you're fearfully and wonderfully made. I know a person that is very close

Donna Floyd
She Can She Will She Wins
Mask Off

to me that is insecure about her weight, and sometimes she would say I wish I were alive. She wanted her life to take a downfall, but I told her that she was beautiful, fearfully, and wonderfully made. I continued to encourage her and let her know that God does not look at the outside, but he looks at the heart. 1st Samuel 16:7| We look and dress up nice, but underneath all that is the issue that we have with ourselves. No matter how we dress or how good we look there is always an issue with us. Sometimes we can look at ourselves in the mirror, and say I look terrible or I'm overweight. We must embrace the skin that we are in because we are jewels in the eyes of the Lord. We worry about what other people think of us, and we fear that we are not good enough, we fear that we will not succeed.

There are so many ways we can overcome, with therapy or the ways of the world, but how I overcame was what God said about me. My healing began when I started speaking about who I am in Christ Jesus. I am fearfully, and wonderfully made. Yes, we all have flaws, no one is perfect, but we serve a perfect God that can change our situations.

My other insecurity was not believing in myself and having that I can't do spirit. I also worried about how people viewed me. I used to wonder if I was good enough for the job. But now, I won't allow my downfalls to determine who I am. We have to stop letting others tell us what we can, or cannot do, whether is it's losing weight or writing a book. The question is how do we overcome these insecurities? How do we love ourselves and find that inner peace?

Donna Floyd
She Can She Will She Wins
Mask Off

The answer:
We have to face the unfaceable, even if we're doing it afraid. Some wounds or scars will never heal. Our past is always something that haunts us. You have to believe in yourself and your dreams. You are somebody. For he who is in you is greater than he that is in the world. You are more than a conqueror through Christ. You are righteous, fearfully, and wonderfully made.
Don't give up, but push through the pain, know that God has the last say so and writes the final chapter. Hold on just a little while longer, if God says it, believe it. Step out there in faith. You have to speak it, believe it, and become it. I cried out to God, and he answered my prayer. Let your pain be your gain. My hiding behind the Mask event, I had a young lady speak about insecurities, a mask that she wore. She described herself as overweight and was abused by her boyfriend emotional and physically. When she spoke, you could tell that she had been delivered. I saw and heard the confidence in her voice as she spoke. She is an overcomer because she believed in who she was. She is a different person today. She has inspired me because I now look in the mirror and say I am fearfully, and wonderfully made.
I used brokenness for usefulness. God will give you strength and power to overcome. We have the victory through Christ Jesus. I used to care about public opinions of how they viewed me. Don't allow others expectation to control you. I had to be who God

Donna Floyd
She Can She Will She Wins
Mask Off

wanted me to be, not what others needed me or wanted me to be.

Sometimes we can be emotionally disconnected until you can be a witness to your pain and speak it. That's when the healing begins. I began to speak things into my life, not how others viewed me but what God thinks about me. I am empowered, equipped, stamped, and approved by God. Don't allow the discouragement over a lack of results keep you from being who you are. Whatever you do, do it all for the glory of God.

Often we avoid doing what's right because of what others might say or think. We must choose to listen to God and not the approval of others. We need to take off the mask of insecurity. God will go before you and open doors that no man can shut. God is my biggest supporter, and he taught me how to believe in myself. He said it's not what you don't know or where you came from, but who you know, and that's Jesus. If you allow others to say you can't, it limits you to what else God wants to do in your life. Press on and tell them to sleep on it.

When I was in the 3rd grade, I overheard my teacher talking to someone about me. She said I needed to attend speech class because I spoke fast, which caused me to stutter. Yes, I talk fast, and yes, sometimes it caused me to stutter. I was insecure about that for a long time. I was afraid to answer my calling because of my speech, but God said it's not your message, but God's message and he can use anyone. The word says God will use the foolish of the world to shame the wise. I know I don't have to

Donna Floyd
She Can She Will She Wins
Mask Off

speak with a large vocabulary to do the work of the Lord. God does not always use the ability, but availabilities. That's why God used little old me to bring his vision to life. The hiding behind the Mask event he used an ordinary person to do extraordinary work to build up his kingdom. I am enough for Jesus. I don't need people to validate me. No matter what others think about you, get up and do it for the Lord and don't allow others to water you down. Don't underestimate yourself, greatness lives in you. Lastly, don't let the possibility of failure keep you from walking in your faith or walking into your purpose. Believe it, speak it and become it. The mask of insecurity is hiding your real and most beautiful self from both ourselves and the world. You are authentic because God made and formed you. Believe what God believes about you.

Do you see yourself as God does? Satan wants you to focus on your failures, but God wants you to focus on your success. You are a diamond, a jewel, blessed, triumphant and beautiful. Mask off

Donna Floyd
She Can She Will She Wins
Mask Off

CHAPTER THREE
Depression

Some depression goes unrecognized, and a lot of times we don't know that we are depressed until something happens to your body. You may have a headache, or you're fatigued, but you would never assume it is depression. I know because I was diagnosed with depression back in 2006. I am not ashamed to tell my story because first of all, it brought healing for me to talk about it. I am a witness to my pain, and now I am set free. Today the joy that I have, I refuse to let anyone or anything take that away. I just decided to walk in my truth with my depression. I started out feeling hopeless and found it hard to get out of bed, and if you're experiencing this, most likely you are depressed.

Depression for many can be complicated and can be hidden so deep that no one recognizes it. When you don't socialize, and you stay to yourself and come up with excuses not to be around anyone, but when you're alone, you don't like it. Then you cover it up and say that you are tired or stressed, but it's bigger than that. But true peace from depression is knowing God is in control, and that he is with you every step of the way. He can shed light on a dark situation. Know that you do not have to struggle alone, we have a Savior that intercedes on our behalf, and when you

Donna Floyd
She Can She Will She Wins
Mask Off

feel discouraged, it is easy to give up but know that Jesus did not give up on you.

Sometimes we get angry when others try to ask us if everything's okay. You respond as if everything is good. We drink or smoke thinking, it will relax us, so we keep sipping, and the next morning the same problems are there.

My husband and I have a blended family, and we have grown to love each other, and I wouldn't trade it for anything. When I first got with my husband, everything was good, but when you are dealing with a blended family, it can get frustrating and complicated. I dealt with baby mama drama, husband drama, kids drama, and family drama.

The church I was attending before I got with my husband was quiet and friendly, but when we got married, I started attending his church faithfully, but I was not living a victorious Christian life. I read my Bible every day because I wanted to serve God even though I was doing these things, I was still miserable most of the time. At this time I was diagnosed with Depression, but today I blame myself for allowing it to happen. You see I wasn't learning how to change. I would go into my room and sit there in the dark sometimes. I was not happy with life, and I was depressed. I would go to church on Sunday and come home and get frustrated with my husband and kids. I felt miserable and unhappy. But I discovered that when we take time to renew our minds with God's word, we learn how to think like Christ. And then we can live a joyful and abundant life. John 10:10| I have come so that you may have life and have it more

Donna Floyd
She Can She Will She Wins
Mask Off

abundantly. Back then, I wasn't trying to hear that because of my unhappiness. My mind was in depression mold, and I was wearing that mask of depression.
Our thoughts and what we say can affect our everyday living and thinking. That's why we have to think like Christ, act like Christ and to be more like Christ, so that we may live an abundant life. God will give you power over your problems, and provide you with control over your flesh.
Know that nothing can separate you from the love of Christ. Romans 8:39| We have to trust God even in an unlikely situation. My depression was so severe that the doctor prescribed Prozac. I had to overcome, so I started digging deeper into the word, and I would go up to Eagle Creek Park by the water and sit there and have a little talk with Jesus. I would dig deep into the word to find a scripture to help me. I would repeat Philippians 4:6 over and over. Do not be worried about anything, but in every situation, pray and petition with thanksgiving, present your request to God and he will give the peace that surpasses all understanding.
I allowed others to walk over me, control me or even slander my name, but God told me to pray for them and love to them.
I would also keep things hidden in me and did not communicate or speak up, and that made it worst. But God did not give us a spirit of fear, but a power of love and a sound mind. 1st Timothy 1:7| One of my favorite scripture is Isaiah 41:10| do not fear, for I am with you, do not be dismayed for I am your God. He

Donna Floyd
She Can She Will She Wins
Mask Off

can turn tragedy into triumph, sorrow to Joy and confusion to peace. I had to continue to run the race and keep my eyes focused on the prize which is Christ Jesus. If we fix our eyes on Jesus, we will not grow weary and lose heart. God's mercy is bigger than all of our problems. He is at my right hand, and I will not be shaken. |Psalms 16-8.

There was this lady that would come up to the clothing store. My husband and I could see that she was going through something and that she was depressed and she didn't know it. Her problem was with her husbands nagging. He would always complain. She would say something's wrong with me like it was her fault. She worked many hours, and she said when she would go home, her husband would take out his anger on her for something that wasn't her fault. She would cook, take care of the kids, and one day she came to work and said, I am tired of being tired, and I am exhausted, I want to give up on life. I said honey you're depressed and the reason why I knew it was depression was that of my bout with it. We must reach out to others and ask what can I do to help the situation, especially if you have been through something that someone else is experiencing. Ask yourself what can I do to improve the situation. We should never be silent about our story, especially if God has delivered you.

We may have rough times, tears, and sorrow, but Joy comes in the morning. God's blessings outweigh life's problems. If you are going through depression, God has not forgotten about you, know that God may

Donna Floyd
She Can She Will She Wins
Mask Off

be preparing you for a breakthrough. God's got you, and even when you don't see it, his grace is still sufficient. I thank God for his vision with Hiding Behind the Mask Conference allowing women to know who they are in Christ Jesus. We all hide, we all have a story that we've never told. Our purpose is to shed our mask and realize we don't have to hide anymore.

We can be disconnected until we are a witness to our pain. I had a young lady speak about depression, and I had a lot of feedback about how they were inspired because she was bold enough to tell her story. Pray and ask God to help you overcome and to give you the wisdom to overcome.

Security in life brings no guarantees, only when we rest in God and his unchanging hand can we find safety. God has a purpose for you, don't give up, but keep the faith. Have the mind of Christ and not the spirit of depression. Mask off.

Donna Floyd
She Can She Will She Wins
Mask Off

Donna Floyd
She Can She Will She Wins
Mask Off

Chapter Four
Addiction

Addiction can be a stressful mask, especially when someone is in denial or disguise. Addiction can be a demon because you are constantly fighting the enemy. It can be alcohol, drugs, sex, even resentment. Dependency can make you hallucinate and can cause your health to deteriorate to the point of death. Like my son and brother, many people suffer from substance abuse or alcohol abuse and live in denial, deception, and delusion. I know my son did for many years. He used to sell it and then became a product of his own drugs. Most people hide behind their mask. Some people have great jobs, benefits, and a lovely home. In this case, they deny that a problem exists in their lives. They downplay the extent of their problem, and when they are by themselves, they face their addiction, but still are in denial telling themselves that they can quit at any time. Their abuse becomes so powerful that they can no longer control it.
Addiction does not have to falter, and addiction is all in your mind and the brain. Addiction can destroy relationships and life. I remember myself enabling my son, I was in denial, but I knew he had a drug problem but did not want to face it. I gave him money for his addiction because I didn't want him out here robbing people. So I would give him money, instead of listening

Donna Floyd
She Can She Will She Wins
Mask Off

to God. I would do the opposite. I was in denial; however self-denial is blinded by addiction, and we don't realize the danger until it's too late. So my son and I both wore the mask and sometimes the mask can be detrimental especially in this case. It was like I was turning away from God in a deliberate act of rejection instead of listening and doing what God said. God will allow suffering to happen in your life if you harden your heart with him. My life was forever changed since my son went home to be with the Lord. God uses me to help others by telling my story. Like I said, addiction is more than just drugs or alcohol. Anything that you allow to control you is an addiction. God wants to deliver you whether it's a substance, thing or activity.

People use drugs or alcohol to escape or reward themselves, but when you suffered enough pain and regret, then you will be ready to stop. My son went through that phase and went through withdrawals. He did not want to hit rock bottom, but as soon as he went back around the drug user, he began to use them again. Bad company corrupts good character. That was the consequence of him going back to the drug which led to his death. The same thing happened to my brother, and he died in his sleep after overdosing. Now there are cases where some people survived addiction, and my husband is one of those people. When I met my husband, he had been drug-free.

Before I end this chapter, I have a testimony about my husband and how he overcame. My husband tells his story as a testimony to let people know there is a remedy and his name is Jesus. In his early years, he sold drugs and eventually that led him to use the

Donna Floyd
She Can She Will She Wins
Mask Off

drugs. My husband is an overcomer, a survivor, and a vessel being used by God to tell his story. His deliverance came about when he cried out to the Lord for help. He was ready to surrender it all to God. God heard his call. My husband sought the Lord, and the Lord heard his cry. Psalm 34:4| I sought the Lord, and he answered me. It was a process for his deliverance, but he stayed in the church and sat at God's feet and continued to serve God.

Today my husband is a Pastor. Won't he do it! Your history does not determine your destiny. It's not where you came from or what you don't know, but who you know which is Christ Jesus. Don't give up even to the point where no one will support you. Know that Jesus is your protector and provider just as he was with my husband. Don't give in, no matter how hard it gets, your breakthrough is on the way. Sometimes things do not work out the way you thought or the way you want them, but know that God has something better for you. If it didn't fall apart, but fell into place, start thanking God for your completion.

God can use anyone, Moses was a murderer, King David was an adulterer and a murderer, Noah was an alcoholic, Rahab was a prostitute, and Paul was a murderer. God can still use you. My husband is a living witness; you have victory through Christ. Mask off.

Donna Floyd
She Can She Will She Wins
Mask Off

Donna Floyd
She Can She Will She Wins
Mask Off

Chapter Five
Abuse

A**buse** can be in the form of physical, mental, and emotional. I had two beautiful ladies speak on this at my last conference, and their deliverance was in the midst of them telling their story. There was a young lady that contacted me after the conference and asked if she could tell her story because of the previous stories she had heard. The speakers talked about being abused as a child. Just think of an image of a little girl hiding behind the mask of abuse. The burden of child abuse is something that no one should have to suffer alone.
The women stood tall and told their stories. It was very inspiring. They no longer hid behind their mask of abuse. They are not just survivors, but warriors that have overcome.

There are cycles of abuse, and each cycle is different, but some people don't realize that one act is no greater than the other.
Domestic violence can happen to anyone regardless if you suffer from emotional, verbal or physical abuse. It can be difficult to understand that someone you love and who claims to love you could abuse you. Emotional abuse is tossed around a lot these days. Emotional abuse is an attempt to control; the only difference is the emotional abuse does not use

Donna Floyd
She Can She Will She Wins
Mask Off

physical kicking, punching or pushing. The abuser continually tries to control your every move.

Emotional abuse can be a painful and a severe pattern of abuse in which the primary effort is to control someone by playing with their emotions.

Verbal insults are the beginning signs of abuse. They start arguing with you and the next thing you know they will call you out of your name. Red flag, I've seen it happen to people I know. Then here comes the physical, first it's a slap, then the hitting. People will only do what you allow them to do. Once you start seeing the signs, that means exit before something tragic happens.

I have a friend that suffered from abused physically, emotionally, and mentally. We have known each other for 25 plus years, and she has a testimony. I hope one day she will tell her story.

Before she came in contact with this guy, she was living her best life. She had it going on, she had a good job, a nice car, and home. She also had a son that endured this abuse as well. She is like family to me. She would come to family gatherings, and she would give you the shirt off her back. She's a lovely and a beautiful lady. One day she met this guy, but there was something about him that I saw way before the incidents started happening. He showed his representative at the beginning. Then he began to change. It started with the yelling and the controlling part. He started calling her out of her name and controlled what she could do. This guy had put a gun to her head and would hit her. I was shocked to see such physical harm.

Donna Floyd
She Can She Will She Wins
Mask Off

We cannot forget these numbers represent real people (my friend) We are hiding the violence behind the mask. It can start as a push and can end up deadly. On the average, nearly 20 people per minute are physically abused by an intimate partner in the United States. 1 in 3 women and 1 in 4 men have been victims of some form of physical violence by their partner. I see it on the news almost every day someone who is the victim of domestic violence. We ignore the signs and then death occurs.

God's power can work miracles. We may have small problems, but our God has big answers. He said I will be with you always, to the end of time. He tells us not to fear or to be afraid; he is our shelter in the time of trouble. Psalms 27| The Lord is the light of my salvation, whom shall I fear, the Lord is the stronghold of my life of whom shall I be afraid. Jesus is the solution to the problems; he is a problem solver and protector. You have to rest in him, knowing God is who he says he is and will do what he says he will do. God is still in control of your situation. What the enemy meant for evil, God meant for good.

We can be so focused on our problems that we neglect the most critical thing, Christ and giving our problems to him. We expect people to meet the needs that only God can fulfill and that loves us unconditionally. We will never be happy physically, emotionally, or mentally until we make God the source of our fulfillment and the answers to our problems. He is the only one who should ever have power over our souls.

Donna Floyd
She Can She Will She Wins
Mask Off

Let's pray, Lord, we look to you for everything and every answer. I pray for healing, I pray for peace and most of all, I pray so that we can put all our expectations in you. We love you and thank you. In Jesus name, we pray. Amen. Mask off

Donna Floyd
She Can She Will She Wins
Mask Off

Chapter 6
Loss of Loved One

A mask can be loneliness or hurt. I've experienced loss, and yes, it is an unbearable pain. I lost my son, brother, and son-in-law within two years of each other. Nobody knows how it feels until you experience the loss. Our grief can be overwhelming, leading to sadness or sinking into depression. We have to get up and face the world every day knowing that our loved one is not here. I know that everyone grieves differently and some grieve longer than others. God has a way of giving you that peace that surpassing all understanding. Even though my biological son's death was more natural to grieve than my son-in-law's and maybe it's how and when it happened. I know the hardest thing I had to do was to tell my grandbaby, his daughter, at the time she was six years old. And when I say, that was the hardest thing to do in my life because she loved her dad. She was a daddy's girl, he did everything for her. He was a great dad, and I know my granddaughter will always remember him.
Shortly after that, the next day in church I could not stop the tears from falling. I cried out to God and asked God why is this so hard for me to take in, and God answered, it's ok because you didn't have time to grieve your son's death, but it's ok my child go ahead and let it out, I am here with you to comfort you.

Donna Floyd
She Can She Will She Wins
Mask Off

Psalm 46:1| God is our refuge and strength, an ever-present help in trouble. Praise be to God and Father of our Lord Jesus Christ, the father of compassion and the God of all comfort. 2nd Corinthians 1-3| Now when my son passed away, God showered peace all on me. I had to pinch myself because it was nobody but God's comfort and peace during the mourning of my son. Glory to God. I remember standing in the hospital waiting room for them to come in, but as I said in the previous chapter, I knew my son had left this world to be with our heavenly father because my heart ached and his heart stopped but everyone else in the waiting room was hoping for a different outcome, but I knew. When the doctors came in and gave us the news, I didn't scream, shout, cry or put my head down. I picked it up because I knew when I got the phone call, don't get me wrong because after the phone call I went in my prayer closet and started praying and crying out to God, but he wouldn't allow me to drop a tear. My God, nobody but God kept me. Even when I lay down at night after the calls, visits, and messages, I was not once restless. The Lord is my shepherd; I should not want. I would repeat that verse over and over again when I did feel grief come over me. God is at my right hand, and I will not be shaken. Psalms 16:8|
Everyone has their way to grieve when it comes to death. I know because I stand on his word and he promises. I have seen what God can do even through the midst of the storm. 2nd Thessalonians 2:15| Stand firm and hold fast to the teachings. Our Lord and Savior love us and by his grace gave us eternal

Donna Floyd
She Can She Will She Wins
Mask Off

encouragement and hope. Encourage our hearts and strengthen us in every good deed and word. When you start sitting at God's feet and have that personal relationship with God, it will be much easier to grieve or to mourn. Because you are reading his word and you know what the word says in time of trials and trouble.

Not everyone acts the same way when it comes to death. There is no reasonable time frame to grieve. s. What hurts the most is that your loved one is not here physically. It's ok to talk about the death of a loved one because denying it is an easy way to isolate yourself from the world. Reach out to others by sharing the good times, and that helps everyone to cope. I remember the next day after my son's passing, I got up and went to the house of the Lord, because I needed the altar prayer for my family and I. The church folks thought I was crazy, here it is 11:00 am, and your son just passed at 10:30 pm.

Nobody but my Lord, that's why I am so in love with the Lord. When I called on him, and he answers, and when I cry to him he says here I am. Anyway, the alter is a part of giving God thanks even through the storms. I had a lady ask me, why are you here? I told her because I serve a God and that God gave me peace that surpasses all understanding. John 14:27| Jesus says my peace I leave with you, my peace I give you. I do not give to you as the world gives. Do not let your hearts be troubled and do not be afraid. When you lose someone the world doesn't understand or know what to say. There was nothing she could have said to make it better, but what she could have

Donna Floyd
She Can She Will She Wins
Mask Off

done was to embrace me with a hug and words of comfort at a time of need. Sometimes that goes over our head. What others need is a hug. Through my son's death, I had to put my trust in God and not in people. Then one day a friend of mine name Vicky called to check on me, she said God wants to use you through your suffering. One of my favorite scripture for suffering is Romans 5:3| Rejoice in suffering because suffering produces endurance, which gives you determination and endurance produces character, which builds you up and character produces hope which is in Christ Jesus. And I was like yes, you are probably right because at your worst that's when God can use you. God speaks through us, through people, circumstances, and his word.
It was May 2015, and my son died in February 2015. I still had not fully understood what God wanted me to do, but my friend called back and said now Donna God wants to use you. So I pray and fast for about two months trying to hear from God. Finally, in August of 2015 is where Hiding Behind the Mask started. Because, you see I wore a mask for almost all my life, a mask of fear, but when my son had passed fear no longer existed. So I was like my mask is off Lord, so how can I be a blessing even when going through it? God did it again. The vision he gave me was to bring women together for healing, just as he healed me and also to let them know who's and who they are in Christ Jesus. As long as I live I will stand on a platform and let women know that they are somebody, no matter what mask you wear. That's why I dedicate my books and event to my son. God

Donna Floyd
She Can She Will She Wins
Mask Off

used him even through his death to accomplish what he is doing today.
God will give you the strength to overcome the loss of a loved one. I use scriptures to help me, and if you believe his promise, he will keep you in perfect peace.
Here are some Scriptures to let you know that your loved ones are still alive in spirit. John 11:25| I am the resurrection and the life. The one who believes in me will live, even though they die, and whoever lives by believing in me will never die. There is life beyond the grave, and I know that my loved one spirit is alive and resting in paradise. Praise God. Revelations 21:4| He will wipe every tear from their eyes. There will be no more death, or mourning, or crying, or pain, for the old things have passed away. They are rejoicing in heaven with no worries. Wow, what a beautiful place to be.
In times of grieving those feelings are yours, and it's ok to cry, grieve, and let it out, but know that with prayer and trust in God he will Comfort you. Suffering is the training ground for Christian's maturity, it develops our patience and makes us stronger. It's ok to celebrate our loved ones to keep the memories alive. I celebrate my son in honor of his life. I celebrate his death, birthday and the event. Just know our loved ones are doing better than us right now, especially in this sinful world. We all have an expiration date, and there is nothing that lives forever but his word. I am going to leave three reasons for suffering.

Donna Floyd
She Can She Will She Wins
Mask Off

1. It reminds us of Christ's suffering on the cross.
2. Keeps us from being Prideful.
3. God's opportunity to demonstrate your pain as a purpose, pain can be your gain.

Step out in faith and let God use you. Mask off.

Donna Floyd
She Can She Will She Wins
Mask Off

Donna Floyd
She Can She Will She Wins
Mask Off

Chapter Seven
Fear

False Things appearing Real = Fear

Fear was my mask. I wore this mask most of my life, even when I was young. If you read my first book, it tells you all about my fears. I was afraid, and I avoided facing fears by hiding behind the mask. I wore a symbolic mask in the hope that I would remain hidden. Fear is what created my mask, and I realize the mask was not who I was, it was hiding my true self, my life was darkness but don't assume the worst. I had a pleasurable childhood, but in realizations, I had that mask of fear until 2015 after my son's death, This is how the hiding behind the mask started. A vision from God and I know he has more to come. He uses a woman who's mask was fear to do extraordinary work to build up his kingdom. Let me give you a little background about my life. First of all, we are born in this world naked and exposed and burnable and dependent on our parents who had us, but God formed us. We take in everything they tell us, and we learn from our mistakes rather; it's our parent's fault or ours. I was very naive and passive growing up, and it was fear that created my mask. I was always the one that would say yes to everything, and I was afraid that people would not like me if I told them no. I was a

Donna Floyd
She Can She Will She Wins
Mask Off

people pleaser. Pretending to be someone that I was not. I wore a mask all the way up until 2015. After going through depression and being controlled, I was even to a point I had to take Prozac for my depression. I felt hurt, lonely and depressed. I hid behind my mask. I was covering it up, and I was seeking and looking in the wrong direction for people, instead of resting in the Lord. I wanted the comfort, the hugs, and the encouragement, but because I put on a fake mask, everyone thought I was ok. I used to agree to what others would say even if it were wrong, and I didn't want them not to like me. If someone wanted to know the truth about themselves, I would lie to make a person like me. I am not ashamed to tell my story because there is a purpose behind my pain and story. I came out of my hiding spot, and it was a process, but because of Christ and knowing who's and who I am in Christ Jesus, I am an overcomer. I have victory today. I used to be a passive woman, no backbone, but a wishbone, but now I am an expected woman. Every day, I get up not waiting for something to happen, but expecting something to happen. I say God is working in my life right now no matter how it looks. I wait in Faith. The antidote for fear is faith. Let me tell you about my calling into the ministry. Now keep in mind God can use anyone and women are very vital in God's ministry today. When I received my calling into the ministry, I was in a church that didn't allow women to preach. So I sat on my calling for years avoiding doing what's right because of what others might think or say. I had a fear of standing up to a person

Donna Floyd
She Can She Will She Wins
Mask Off

even if it was right. As I said before in the previous chapter, I speak fast sometimes, and I stumble over my words. I was more afraid to speak in front of people, but if God called you, God will give you the ability to complete the task. God told me you don't have to be a great speaker with a large vocabulary to speak or to share the gospel. Just like Moses wasn't a great speaker, but God said, isn't I the one who made your tongue and Moses became a great leader. The power is in the story. I realize focusing on other peoples opinion can distract you from your destiny. If you depend on people to love or support you the way God does, you will always be disappointed. I expected people to do what only God can do and that was to love me unconditionally. I had to step into my destiny and not be afraid or worry about what others thought. I had to shift my focus on Christ and off other people. I used to be afraid what others thought, but God said that I am equipped, empowered and approved by him. I stop settling for less than Gods highest best for me. You can do all things through Christ Jesus who strengthens you. Philippians 4-13| Don't ever underestimate yourself because greatness lives in you. The antidote for fear is faith. Faith is a mindset that expects God to act and when we act on expectation, we can overcome fear. It's crazy because we think that we might have it beat, but it creeps back up on you. I just experienced a life-changing encounter with God back in October 25th of 2018. I needed a vacation at that time, because of life circumstances that I was going through, especially since Satan was attacking my

Donna Floyd
She Can She Will She Wins
Mask Off

marriage and children. So I traveled to the Joyce Meyer's Love Women's Conference alone to Tampa, Florida. I've never traveled alone in my life, but it was all designed and set up just the way God planned it and designed it. As I embarked on the fear that weekend, I came out stronger and fearless than ever in my life. Letting something go and taking hold of something new. New transformation, different mindset. I had to find me again, but it was all for a great comeback. I had an encounter with God in my hotel room. The getaway was all set up by God himself. I was supposed to travel with friends, but that didn't work out because God already predestined this trip. As I was praying and talking to God, his spirit came over me, and I felt the presence of the Lord. I started crying out to the Lord and praying, and as I stopped and listened to God. God told me I am waiting for you. I've been praying to God about what to do, and he said, I am waiting for you. He's already giving you all you need to work with, so never underestimate the power that's in you. You have to tap into it. God qualifies you and anoints you not people. What I am trying to say is I felt a wedge between God and I, and I allowed fear and opinions of others to dictate who I was in Christ. 2nd Timothy 1:7| For God has not given us a spirit of fear, but of power, love and a sound mind. My mind is free, and I realize if I were here to please people I would not be a servant of Christ Jesus. To please God, you may have to disappoint some people. He called me, and he anoints me, He gives me the power to do all things. God is our source of spiritual strength. So I know

Donna Floyd
She Can She Will She Wins
Mask Off

what to do now. Keep pushing, people may pressure me, but my purpose is to follow the calling God has placed upon me. Do it even when you are afraid. When I tell you that I am on fire for the Lord and not caring what others think or say. It started fearlessly traveling alone. What's lost now is found, and that's the anointing spirit that was never gone. It was always there I just had to tap into it. The enemy will try to pull you from God. And tell you that you're not good enough or make you feel less. Whose life are you living? Do you want to be accepted by many or commit and follow God? Do not allow anything or anyone to extinguish what God is doing in you. I started looking at myself differently, realizing it was right there. Inside of me is the same power that rose Jesus from the dead. The wonderful power of the holy spirit is the word of wisdom
I had to stop being afraid and being a people pleaser, so I had to leave behind others to gain God's approval. Don't miss your destiny. Sometimes you have to lose everything to become God's everything.

Donna Floyd
She Can She Will She Wins
Mask Off

Donna Floyd
She Can She Will She Wins
Mask Off

How to Shed your Mask

Awareness: Admitting and taking the first step to grow into your potential.

Realization: We have to realize who we are, you are somebody, you are a diamond, a jewel, you're awesome, you're blessed, triumphant, and you are a child of the most high. Don't look at how you think you should be, but let the world know who you are. Last but not least, healing to speak, to tell your story. Nothing different will happen if you don't do it differently. It's time to break free, even if you have to do it afraid. The devil wants you to focus on your failure. He wants you to feel little about yourself. You are fearfully and wonderfully made. You are that woman, and you need to set her FREE. Mask off

Donna Floyd
She Can She Will She Wins
Mask Off

NOTES:

Donna Floyd
She Can She Will She Wins
Mask Off

www.ingramcontent.com/pod-product-compliance
Lightning Source LLC
Chambersburg PA
CBHW051710090426
42736CB00013B/2639